Ten-Minute Real World Writing

by Murray Suid
illustrated by Philip Chalk

This book is for
Eric Dorsey

Publisher: Roberta Suid
Editor: Carol Whiteley
Production: Scott McMorrow

Other Monday Morning publications by the author: *Book Factory,
For the Love of Research, How to Be an Inventor, How to Be President of
the U.S.A., Picture Book Factory, Report Factory, Storybooks Teach Writing,
Ten-Minute Grammar Grabbers, Ten-Minute Editing Skill Builders, Ten-
Minute Thinking Tie-ins, Ten-Minute Whole Language Warm-ups*

■ E-mail address: MMBooks@aol.com ■

Entire contents copyright © 1996 by Monday Morning Books, Inc.,
Box 1680, Palo Alto, CA 94302

For a complete catalog, please write to the address above.

ISBN 1-57612-000-7

Printed in the United States of America
9 8 7 6 5 4 3 2 1

Contents

INTRODUCTION

Writing takes dozens of forms. An anecdote, for example, has a different structure than an essay. A thank-you note is nothing like a character sketch or a song lyric.

This variety can evoke a river of creativity. But to take advantage of it, students must be taught the nuts and bolts of each type of writing.

Ten-Minute Starting Points

Complete mastery of any type of writing takes years. But a meaningful introduction to a given form requires only a few minutes. This book will help you get the process underway.

In the following pages, you'll find lessons for teaching 30 formats. The formats are called "real world" because people use them throughout their lives. For example, most of us have passed out flyers or sent thank-you notes.

The projects are not only "real," they also offer practice in both nonfiction and fiction areas. Thus, after writing Thank-you Notes for pretend gifts, students might write notes for real gifts they have received.

The Lessons

Each lesson begins with a definition or background information. Models accompany unusual formats such as Cliffhangers.

Simple, step-by-step directions tell how to move through each writing practice. A key step calls for sharing drafts in small groups. This allows young writers to feel pride in their efforts, while seeing how their work is received. Professional writers often participate in groups for the same reasons.

Beyond Ten Minutes

Following each introductory lesson is an extension activity that enables students to apply what they learned in greater depth. The extension may include revising a draft, adding art, and publishing the result as part of a class-made book.

If your students need practice in the skill of revising, you might wish to take a look at two other books in this series: *Ten-Minute Editing Skill Builders* and *Ten-Minute Grammar Grabbers*.

Bonus Section

The Resources section at the end of the book begins with a reproducible Writer's Guide, which offers many practical tips on topics ranging from writing interesting leads to creating dialogue.

This section also includes an illustrated lesson for students on publishing books: covers, typography, art, and binding.

Many teachers believe that evaluation is the key to making progress as a writer. You'll find two pages of suggestions for teaching students to evaluate their own work and the work of their peers.

There's also a primer on e-mail and the Internet for teachers not yet familiar with cyberspace. E-mail is an exciting development because it has renewed interest in letter writing, which is one of the best activities known for developing literacy skills. Along with definitions and suggested activities, you'll find a list of interesting e-mail and World Wide Web addresses, plus an invitation to share your discoveries with us.

The Bibliography lists familiar books that can be used as models for exploring some of the formats covered by the lessons.

Where to Begin

Each kind of writing offers unique opportunities for sharing ideas and information. There truly is no one right place to begin. That's why the book is organized alphabetically. You might start at the beginning, or you might prefer to zero in on a format that ties into a lesson in another part of your curriculum. For example, Walking Tours, page 76, can be used for making science reports.

The Best Writing Resource

Many factors influence whether or not a child learns to love writing. Being read to is important. Having real reasons to write makes a difference, as when older children write stories that will actually be read by younger students.

But the single most important strategy for creating able young writers is to make sure they see an admired adult writing on a regular basis. For many students, that person is the teacher. If you try the activities with students and share your efforts, you will have done a great deal to put them on the road to literacy.

ANECDOTES

An anecdote is a short, entertaining story. While often based on a real happening, the truth may be "stretched" for the sake of humor or drama.

DIRECTIONS:

1. Introduce the format by telling an anecdote from your life or by reading the model on the next page.
2. Ask students to brainstorm funny or dramatic incidents from their lives. These might be stories told and retold at family gatherings. To jog students memories, post anecdote topics, such as those listed in the margin.
3. Have students draft short accounts of their anecdotes.
4. Share the stories in small groups.

EXTENSION:

Create a class book of anecdotes. Students should polish their drafts, then add illustrations.

Anecdote Topics
Accidents
Breaking things
Chores
Eating
Emergencies
Family reunions
Finding things
First times
Getting lost
Gifts (odd)
Going somewhere
Learning something
Losing things
Making things
Seeing things

Anecdote Model

Stuck in the Mud

Mud isn't just dirty. It's nasty. I learned that the hard way.

We had recently moved into a newly built house in a block of other new houses. The place had been a chicken farm before the houses were built. There wasn't any grass, only dirt. When rain started, the dirt became mud.

My parents told me not to go outside because I'd ruin my clothes. But after a few days of rain I was bored staying inside. I asked, "If I wear old clothes, can I go out and play?"

"OK," said my mom. "But don't stay out too long."

I put on my oldest clothes and high rubber boots, and went out into the back yard. Each time I took a step, the thick and squishy mud gripped my boot. Suddenly, one boot got stuck. I couldn't move it. I pushed down on the other foot, and it got stuck, too. I was caught like an animal in a trap.

It seemed as if an hour passed before my mom came to the door and shouted, "Didn't I tell you to come in soon?"

"I can't," I said. "The nasty old mud won't let me."

My dad finally rescued me by pulling me out of the boots and leaving the boots stuck in the mud. We never did find them. Maybe the mud ate them up!

AUTOBIOGRAPHIES

An autobiography needs a theme. For example, in an artist's autobiography, a chapter on education would likely focus on learning to draw.

DIRECTIONS:
1. Explain that autobiographies are stories that people write about themselves. ("Auto" means self. The first cars were called automobiles because they were self-propelled, rather than drawn by horses.)
2. Have students complete the Autobiographical Planner on the following page. The sixth question is important because titles can help a writer focus. Examples of clarifying titles are "My Life as a Saxophone Player" or "The Story of a Stamp Collector."
3. If time permits, students can share their filled-in planners in small groups.

EXTENSION:
Have students use their Autobiographical Planners to write autobiographies. For an imaginative twist, students can write "Future Autobiographies," envisioning what they hope to become. Or they might write fictional autobiographies that tell the stories of things—"My Life as an Alarm Clock"—or animals—"I'm a Happy Gerbil."

I don't know what to write about in my autobiography.

Autobiographical Planner

The following questions can help you prepare to write an autobiography: the story of your life. If you need more space to write your answers, use the back or another piece of paper.

1. What activity is most important to you? Think about hobbies, school subjects, sports, clubs you belong to, and so on.

_____

2. How did you become interested in the activity? For example, did you read about it or learn about it from a friend?

_____

3. Who taught you the most about the activity?

_____

4. Why do you like the activity?

_____

_____

5. What goals do you have concerning your skill? For example, a magician might want to perform on TV.

_____

_____

6. What title will your autobiography have? _Hint_: Titles often have seven or fewer words, for example, "My Tuba and Me."

_____

BIOGRAPHIES

The first step in writing a biography is choosing a subject worth writing about. The person needn't be famous, but someone the writer considers interesting.

DIRECTIONS:

1. Explain that a biography is a true story about a person other than the writer. A biography may cover many topics, including family history and education. But there usually will be a specific focus, for example, a major achievement or an attribute such as courage.

2. Have students list three or more possible biographical subjects: relatives, friends, neighbors, or pets treated as people. *Note*: Although professional biographers often write about strangers, doing so requires extensive research.

3. Students should choose the most interesting person on their lists and, in small groups, explain why the chosen subject is memorable.

EXTENSION:

Have students write biographies of their subjects after gathering information by tapping their own memories; by interviewing people familiar with the subjects; and/or by studying letters, photos, and other artifacts. For a biography model, see the following page.

Biography Model

Dumb Dog or Clever Canine?

Spice is our cocker spaniel. Her mother and her father were champions. They were not only beautiful dogs, but also extremely intelligent.

On the day we brought Spice home from the kennel, my brother and I discussed all the neat tricks we would teach her. We expected that she would go on TV and make us famous.

Ten years later, Spice has learned exactly zero tricks. She won't sit up if you ask her to. She won't roll over. She won't heel or fetch. She will bark if she's hungry or wants to go out for a walk, but we didn't teach her to do that.

When Spice first refused to learn any tricks, we took stacks of dog books out of the library and followed the directions step by step. Nothing worked. One day, we saw an advertisement in which a dog trainer said he "could teach any dog to obey." After a month of lessons, the trainer kicked Spice out of the class. The trainer's advertisement now reads "I can teach <u>almost</u> any dog to obey."

All our friends say that Spice is just plain dumb, but as the years go by, she seems happier than ever. She gets her way every time. Maybe she's the smartest one in our family.

BRAINSTORMING

Edison tested dozens of items before finding the right filament for his bulb. Picasso made sketch after sketch before painting a canvas. All kinds of creative people seek many possible solutions to a problem. This requires mental flexibility; brainstorming is a good way to get it.

DIRECTIONS:
1. Teach the two main brainstorming strategies:
   - Work quickly.
   - Write down every thought. Don't worry about wrong or silly answers. The goal is quantity.
2. Give students a brainstorming starter, for example, "Name at least ten objects that can be used as a chair." See the next page for other examples.
3. Have students, working alone or with a partner, write their thoughts.
4. Share the results in small groups or in a large group.
5. Repeat the activity frequently. You might ask students to suggest their own brainstorming starters.

EXTENSION:
When giving formal assignments, find ways to work in brainstorming. For example, have students brainstorm at least five titles for a paper, and then choose the best.

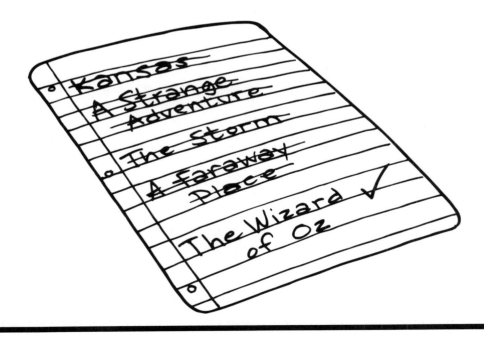

Brainstorming Starters

For each item, the brainstormer lists as many examples as possible. Alternatively, there can be a goal, e.g., "Ten animals that wouldn't make good pets."

- Words starting or ending with "A" (or any letter)
- Things made of glass
- Uses for objects other than their intended uses, for example:
    a shoe could be a house for a mouse
    a sock could be a puppet
- Things in your house that you could easily live without
- Words that mean more to your parent or guardian than to you
- Activities that you do that no one did 100 years ago
- Activities people will do in 100 years that aren't done now
- Hiding places for an elephant (a bird, a snake)
- Reasons why you would (would not) want to be:
    a book
    a mirror
    a movie star
    a shark
    a tree
- Questions you can't answer
- Reasons for:
    asking questions
    reading a book
    watching TV
- Things that don't break when you drop them

CAPTIONS

A picture may be worth a thousand words. But a picture with an informative caption will be even more valuable.

DIRECTIONS:

1. If students aren't familiar with the concept of the caption, pass out the model on page 15 and discuss the two main elements:
   - An opening phrase that functions as a headline and that often appears in boldface letters
   - Names and/or dates that can't be learned from the picture, and other background information

2. Give students a picture without a caption, for example, an image from page 16 or 17.

3. Have students, working alone or with a partner, study the picture and draft a 25- to 30-word caption for it. Students should make up names and other information, or have the class brainstorm the "facts" ahead of time.

4. Share the captions orally in small groups.

EXTENSION:

Ask students to include pictures and captions in a science, social studies, or writing assignment. The pictures can be originals or ones adapted from a publication, in which case the original sources should be credited.

Caption Model

MINIATURE GOLF—originally called "Tom Thumb" golf—was invented by John Carter in the 1920s, about 500 years after regular golf was first played. The Chattanooga, Tennessee, inventor named his game in honor of General Tom Thumb, a famous circus midget. Although Carter's invention became popular, the term "Tom Thumb" was replaced by "miniature," a word used to describe many other things including transistor radios and even poodles.

Realistic Pictures to Caption

CHARACTER SKETCHES

Some writers like to think about their characters before starting on a story. They do this by making up information about their characters as if the characters were alive.

DIRECTIONS:
1. Choose a famous storybook character, or have the class choose one.
2. Pass out the Character Checklist, page 19.
3. Have students, working alone or with a partner, complete the checklist for the character chosen.
4. Share the results. Expect big differences, because character analysis is more of an art than a science.

EXTENSION:
Have students use the Character Checklist when creating characters for their own stories.

Character Checklist

Fill in the following information for a character. Use the back of this paper to add other details.

Title of story: _____

Character's name: _____

Character's age: _____

Appearance. First thing you'd notice:
( ) eyes
( ) hair
( ) mouth
( ) clothing
( ) other _____

Activities:
( ) plays chess
( ) collects _____
( ) cooks
( ) dances
( ) draws
( ) listens to _____ music
( ) performs magic tricks
( ) plays an instrument _____
( ) reads (type of book) _____
( ) job
( ) other _____

Personality:
( ) brave
( ) confident
( ) cooperative
( ) friendly
( ) honest
( ) intelligent
( ) nasty
( ) nervous
( ) serious
( ) silly
( ) other _____

Quirks:
( ) frowns often
( ) smiles often
( ) snaps fingers
( ) wears something odd _____
( ) whistles often
( ) other _____

Weaknesses:
( ) can't keep a secret
( ) always late
( ) other _____

Favorites:
( ) food _____
( ) friend _____
( ) place _____
( ) other _____

CLIFFHANGERS

Cliffhangers, such as the "Perils of Pauline," helped movies become a popular entertainment medium. This format can stimulae your students' creativity.

DIRECTIONS:

1. Explain that a cliffhanger is a story that has a thrilling climax. Usually, the hero or someone the hero cares for is in great danger. The trick is getting the person out of danger. If students are unfamiliar with the format, share the Cliffhanger Model on page 23.
2. Read the class a Cliffhanger Story Card from the next page.
3. Have students, alone or in small groups, brainstorm solutions. To promote inventiveness, ban the "And-then-I-woke-up!" ending. It's a cliché.
4. Share the solutions orally.
5. For more practice, have students write stories inspired by the Cliffhanger Picture Cards on page 22.

EXTENSION:

Have students create text or picture cliffhanger starters to swap with classmates.

Cliffhanger Story Cards

The Boa Had Me

The boa constrictor wrapped itself tighter and tighter around me. I could hardly breathe.

If only I could get the attention of my friends in the nearby cabin. Unfortunately, I didn't have enough air inside my lungs to shout or even whisper.

The Ledge

I live on the fifth floor of an old high-rise apartment building.

This morning, chirping woke me. I looked out my window and saw a baby bird trembling in a nearby nest. A large cat was climbing toward it.

A narrow ledge runs past my window. From there, I could scare the cat. Out I went. But while I was chasing away the cat, the window shut.

Broken Brakes

I love speed. Someday I'd like to fly rockets. But that would be far in the future...if I had a future.

At the moment, I was zooming down Main Street Hill at 30 miles per hour. For those of you who know metrics, that's 48 kilometers per hour.

The brakes on my 10-speed had failed. Two blocks straight ahead was the stone wall that ran along the creek.

Cliffhanger Model

The Boulder Race

I was climbing Tall Mountain when an earthquake shook the ground. At first, I was glad to be outside. No building could fall on me. Then I heard a horrible noise. Near the peak, a dozen boulders had broken loose and were rolling toward me, knocking over giant pines as if the trees were pencils.

I ran down the hill, but the boulders were gaining speed. They'd be impossible to dodge because there was almost no space between them. I once read about someone in a similar jam who had crawled into a hole. The stones had rolled right over the person. Unfortunately, I could see no holes ahead of me, only trees, and they couldn't protect me.

Wait! Maybe they could, but I would have to act fast. The boulder was just seconds away. I climbed the nearest tree. When I came to a limb, I moved out on it.

The biggest boulder aimed right at my tree. I counted the seconds. Just before the boulder hit, I leaped from the branch onto the rolling stone. I ran in the direction that the stone was turning. I was like one of those trained circus seals that walks on a beach ball as it moves across the stage.

The rock ball I was moving on was going downhill faster than a speeding train. I was huffing and puffing, but I was thankful that the stone hadn't rolled on top of me. Before I could enjoy my good luck too much, I looked ahead and saw that the boulder was heading directly toward a cliff. If it went over, it would fall a mile down. I didn't like that thought at all. What could I do?

COMICS

Comic strips and comic books were perfected in the twentieth century. However, the tradition of combining pictures and words can be traced to the scientific drawings of Michelangelo, and even further back to storytelling tapestries of the Middle Ages.

DIRECTIONS:
1. Give each student or pair of students the comic starter on the next page.
2. Have students fill in the dialogue balloons to complete the story. Point out that there is no one right way to do this. A hundred writers might do the job a hundred different ways. Students might include narration at the top of one or more panels. (See the example below.)
3. Share the student work through oral readings or by posting the fill-in comics on a bulletin board.
4. To give practice in using comics for nonfiction, have students fill in the comic on page 26.

EXTENSION:
This activity can be endlessly repeated by covering up the balloons in comics found in the newspaper or in books. To help students who wish to draw their own comics, duplicate the drawing tips on page 27.

Comic Fill-in: Fiction

Study the pictures to figure out what the story is about. Then fill in the dialogue that each character is saying. Print a title on the title line.

_____

(title line)

Comic Fill-in: Nonfiction

Comics can be used to make reports, teach skills, and present other true information. After studying the pictures, fill in the dialogue.

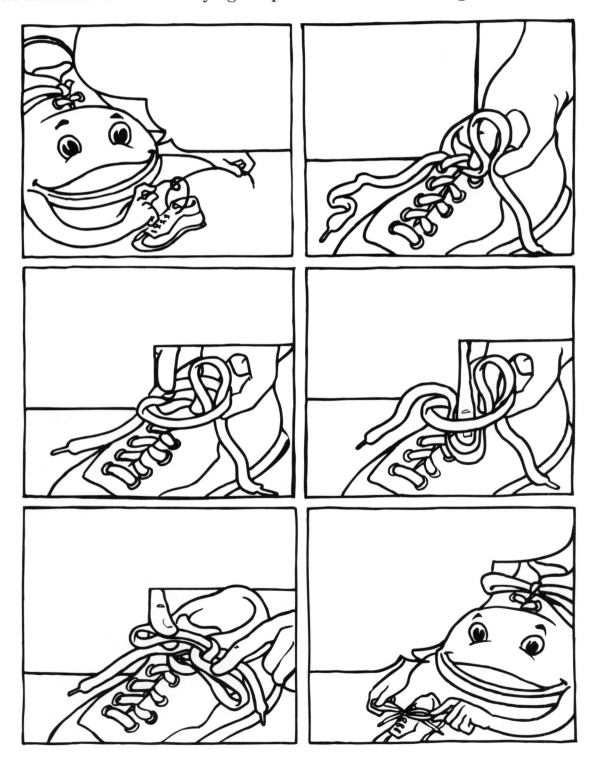

1 Divide the page into panels before you start, and use a pencil so you can erase any mistakes.

2 Sketch the items to be drawn. Leave space if you plan to include narration and dialogue.

NARRATION BOX

DIALOGUE BOX

3 You can make your drawings cartoon-like or realistic.

You don't want to bite me! I don't even taste good!

BARK BARK

4 When you're done, go over the pencil lines in ink. Then erase the pencil lines.

You don't want to bite me! I don't even taste good!

BARK BARK BARK BARK

CONTEST ENTRIES

Remember those once-popular contests in which people tried to win a prize by stating an opinion in 25 words or less? In the classroom, this mini-essay challenge boasts a greater reward: mastering the art of conciseness.

DIRECTIONS:
1. Give students a topic that they are familiar with. It should involve stating and justifying an opinion.
2. Ask students to write a few sentences about the topic (see possible contest topics on the next page). If you're working with advanced writers, you might require an essay of exactly 25 words.
3. Have students share their writing in small groups, or post revised versions on a bulletin board.

EXTENSION:
Create a class book of essays on the same topic.

Contest Topics

Note: The writer should first fill in the blank with a name or phrase and then write the essay.

I wish everyone could meet _____ because...

The most exciting moment in my life was _____ because...

The most useful thing I ever learned is _____ because...

I'd like to visit _____ because...

The best book I ever read was _____ because...

The most important word is _____ because...

The best luck I ever had was _____ because...

The secret of friendship is _____ because...

If I had to be an object, I'd be a (an) _____ because...

_____ is my favorite season because...

The best way to deal with failure is _____ because...

I wish I could understand _____ because...

Reading is important to me because...

The best holiday is _____ because...

I'd like to switch places with _____ because...

I'd like to read _____ 's mind because...

If I had a million dollars, I'd use it to _____ because...

I'd like to learn how to _____ because...

If I could change one thing in the world, I'd change _____ because...

I'd like to be the first person ever to _____ because...

The skill I'm proudest of is _____ because...

DEFINITIONS

Nonfiction writers often create original definitions to help readers understand their subjects. The task of defining things provides strong practice in analytical thinking and descriptive writing.

DIRECTIONS:

1. Choose a subject to define. It should be a familiar object or activity, for example, the telephone or the game of softball.
2. Ask students to write a definition of about 50 words. Writers should pretend that they are explaining the subject to someone who has never heard of it. Defining an activity, such as football, may involve a list of chronological steps.
3. Have students share their definitions in small groups.
4. For more practice, use the list on the next page, or have the students choose subjects from their own lives.

EXTENSION:

Have students include original definitions in some of their reports. You might later publish these definitions in a class-made dictionary.

Subjects to Define

Animal
Baseball (and other games)
Dream
Experiment
Family
Fire drill
Friend
Habit
Hand
Homework
Job
Long division
Movie
Music
Nightmare
Pet
Rain
School
Science
Skateboarding
Sleep
Smell
Smile
Sunshine
Teacher
Television
Thinking
Thunder
Water
Wind

DESCRIPTIVE WRITING

Descriptive writing aims to create a picture in the reader's mind. The process has two steps: first, seeing or imagining the object; second, finding details that enable the reader to see the object.

DIRECTIONS:
1. To help students grasp the concept of descriptive writing, read them one of the passages on the following page. Each passage is accompanied by a simple picture.
2. Ask students to draw a picture of what they "see" as they hear the description.
3. Draw the picture on the board.
4. Have students compare their pictures with the one you drew. Discuss the differences, going back to the text as necessary.
5. Later, repeat the practice using the other descriptions on page 33, or using examples created by students.

EXTENSION:
To help students focus on details, have them compare and contrast the related subjects pictured on pages 34 and 35. Augment those examples with pairs of actual objects such as apples or pieces of chalk.

Descriptive Passages

The two-story house sat on the top of a hill that was so tall it was among the clouds. The front door of the house was on the left. To the right of the door was a wide picture window. There were two bedrooms upstairs, each with a window facing the front. On top of the flat roof sat an old bicycle. It had been there for so long, no one could remember who put it on the roof, or why.

At first, the clock seemed ordinary: a round face set in a wooden square frame. But then I looked closer. Instead of numbers, it had letters. A capital A was where the 12 usually would be. B was where the number 1 should have been, and so on around the face. Instead of two hands, there were three. The longest pointed to the E, the next longest pointed at the H, and the shortest pointed at the L. I had no idea how to tell what time it was.

Suddenly, a large fish sprang from the water, pointing straight up. It had a long, sword-like nose, a large fin on its back, and a small fin on its belly. To the right was a half moon.

Things to Compare and Contrast

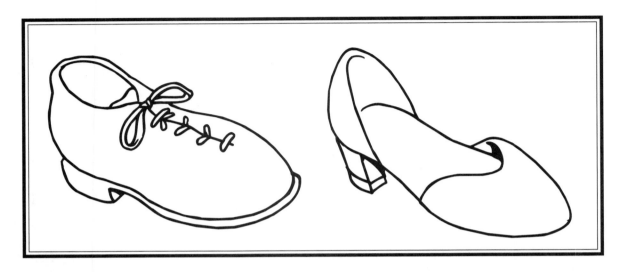

DIALOGUES

The dialogue is a read-aloud play in which two characters discuss a topic. The format was made famous by Plato thousands of years ago, but is simple enough for students to use to explore ideas.

DIRECTIONS:

1. Choose, or have students choose, a pair of familiar characters who would have something to say to each other:
- Fictional characters (the Hare and the Tortoise)
- Real characters (historical or contemporary)
- Vocational types (a doctor and a lawyer)
- Personified objects (a pear and an orange)

For more ideas, see the following page.

2. Have students write brief imaginary conversations between the characters. The speaker's name precedes each speech.

3. Students can share their work in small groups. While the author listens, two students perform the dialogue.

EXTENSION:

Use this format for research reports. After gathering facts, students write the information as a dialogue.

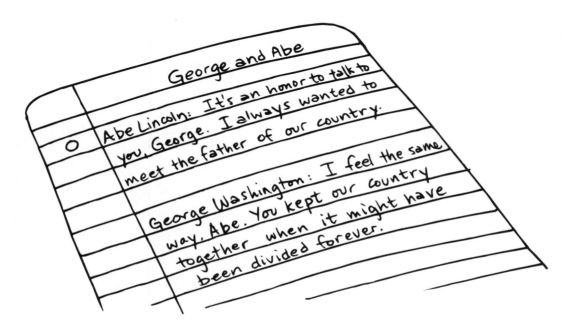

George and Abe

Abe Lincoln: It's an honor to talk to you, George. I always wanted to meet the father of our country.

George Washington: I feel the same way, Abe. You kept our country together when it might have been divided forever.

Characters for Dialogues

In the following examples, the two participants might compare notes, debate whose life is better, explain their functions or histories, or otherwise chat about their respective points of view.

Animals: e.g., a bird and a worm

Body parts: e.g., an eye and an ear

Cities: e.g., two world capitals, or a big city and a village

Countries: e.g., Mexico and Canada

Emotions: e.g., crying and laughing

Exercises: e.g., jogging and swimming

Foods: e.g., a pizza and a taco

Government: e.g., President and Prime Minister

Inventions: e.g., a ballpoint pen and a computer

Letters: e.g., a vowel and a consonant

Musical instruments: e.g., a piano and a drum

Natural phenomena: e.g., lightning and wind

Numbers: e.g., an even number and an odd number

Pastimes: e.g., scouting and stamp collecting

People: e.g., a baby and an elementary school student

Pets: e.g., a cat and a dog

Planets: e.g., Jupiter and Mars

School subjects: e.g., art and science

Seasons: e.g., summer and winter

Sports: e.g., a football player and a soccer player

Time: e.g., day and night

Transportation devices: e.g., a train and a plane

DIARIES

"Diary" comes from a Latin word meaning "day." Keeping a diary is a powerful way to practice storytelling on a daily basis. Although the format can be used to write about one's own life, it is also a way to retell classic stories.

DIRECTIONS:

1. If students aren't familiar with the diary format, read them the example on the following page. Point out the two elements that are commonly found in diaries:
   - The writing is done in the first person (I).
   - The events are told in the simple past tense.

2. Choose a well-known short story. It could be a fairy tale "Cinderella," a fable "The Hare and the Tortoise," a parable, or any other story students are familiar with.

3. Have students choose a character from the story and write a diary entry from the character's point of view. If the story covers more than one day, students could have the option of focusing on one incident or writing several entries, each under a different day.

EXTENSION:

In addition to giving students time to keep their own diaries, you might have them use the format to create unusual diary book reports.

Rumpelstiltskin's Diary

Sunday:

I'm in a good mood today. I overheard a peasant bragging that his daughter could spin straw into gold. The king loves gold and immediately put the girl into a room with lots of straw. He told her she could marry his son if she spun the straw into gold. But she would die if she couldn't do it.

As soon as the king closed the door, I magically appeared in a cloud of smoke. This frightened her, of course. People are always surprised when I magically appear. I like scaring them.

When the woman got over the surprise of seeing me, she started to tell me her problem. Because I already knew it, I interrupted her and offered to help her if she promised to give me the bracelet she was wearing. She agreed, and I spun the straw into gold.

She was so happy she didn't notice my sly grin. I know what's going to happen next, but she doesn't. She'll find out soon enough, and I'll write about it here as soon as it happens.

DREAMS

Even though everyone dreams, writing fictional dreams requires creativity and effort.

DIRECTIONS:
1. List a few famous story dreams, for example, Alice's Wonderland dream, Dorothy's Oz dream, and Max's dream of where the Wild Things live.
2. Ask students to suggest common dream elements. These might include:
- A strange setting
- Odd characters
- Changes in the laws of nature
- Unconnected events
- Repeated events

3. Have students write fictional dreams. They should use the first person and the present tense. For ideas, see the list of dreamers on the next page or the Dream Starter picture cards on pages 42 and 43.

EXTENSION:
Have students write and illustrate stories in which dreams play an important part.

Dream Starters: Dreamers

Human Dreamers
Artist
Athlete
Baby
Inventor
Movie star
Painter
Police officer
President or Prime Minister
Scientist
Shy person
Singer
Soldier
Taxicab driver
Teacher

Animal Dreamers (personified)
Ant
Cat
Dinosaur
Dog
Parrot
Snake
Spider
Whale

Object Dreamers (personified)
Airplane
Book
Bottle
Clock
Cloud
Doll house
Hammer
Key
Number
Pencil
Robot
Telephone
Truck

FLYERS

Have you ever lost a set of keys or found a lost cat? One of the best ways to communicate this kind of neighborhood news is by creating an eye-catching mini-poster.

DIRECTIONS:
1. Brainstorm a list of things people lose or find.
2. Pass out copies of the flyer model on the next page. Discuss the elements:
- Headline
- Artwork
- Details
- Phone number
3. Have students choose one of the lost or found items on the list and draft a flyer for it.
4. Share the flyers in small groups or on a bulletin board.

EXTENSION:
Try the same activity using imaginary items such as a pet dinosaur, a household robot, a talking tomato, or something from a favorite book, for example, the magic slippers from The Wizard of Oz or the Cheshire Cat from Alice's Adventures in Wonderland.

STOLEN:

HEADLINE →

GOOSE

THAT LAID GOLDEN EGGS

ART →

TEXT →

My goose was stolen last Thursday. The thief was a boy named Jack. He was last seen climbing down the big beanstalk outside of town. If you see the goose, Jack, or any golden eggs, please call 555-1234 day or night. <u>Big reward</u>: <u>three golden eggs</u>!

HOW TO DO IT

Everybody's an expert on something. By sharing our various skills, we can create a more intelligent, more able community.

DIRECTIONS:

1. If students haven't written skill directions before, read them the model on the next page. Go over the elements:
   • Title
   • Introduction that motivates the reader
   • Step-by-step explanation in chronological order
   • Pictures as needed
2. Have students brainstorm skills they've mastered, which could be taught in a few steps. How to play the piano is probably too big a topic, but how to practice the piano might work.
3. Have each student choose a skill and list the steps involved.
4. Later, have students write and illustrate lessons teaching their skills.

EXTENSION:

Use the same format for doing reports in which students personify animals or inventions and explain how they work.

The first step in spinning a web is....

How-to Article Model

How to Take a "Natural" Photograph

Many photographs make people look stiff and uncomfortable as they face the camera and say "Cheese." The question is: How can we show our friends and family members the way they really are? Here's the answer.

Step 1.   Be sure you know how to use the camera.

Step 2.   Make sure the camera has film in it.

Step 3.   Ask the person you want to photograph to find an activity he or she often does.

Step 4.   Don't be in a hurry to take the photograph. At first, your subject may be stiff, but after a few minutes he or she will begin to relax, especially if you don't stand too close or call attention to the camera.

Step 5.   If the person looks toward you, ask him or her to focus on the activity at hand, not at the camera.

Step 6.   Take more than one photograph. Try different positions.

INTRODUCTIONS

Every public speaker deserves an intelligent introduction, one that prepares the audience for the speech.

DIRECTIONS:
1. Make sure students understand what an introduction is. You might read them the example on page 49.
2. Go over the key points found in most introductions, though not necessarily in this order:
   • A lead that tells about the speaker's job or interest
   • A preview of what will be in the speech
   • A description of the speaker's background
   • A greeting to the speaker ("Now here is Mr. Suid.")
3. Have students choose someone they know and write a one-minute introduction for a speech that person might give.
4. Students can share their introductions in small groups.

EXTENSION:
As part of an oral report assignment, have students buddy up. Each partner will find out what the other is going to say, then write and give an introduction. This way, the amount of public speaking practice is doubled.

Introduction Model

Meet a Plumber

If you go to the movies, you don't usually see a plumber as the hero. Yet in everyday life, plumbers often come to the rescue. They solve all sorts of problems, from little drips to major floods. They answer calls on weekends, at nights, and in storms. Their work can be dirty, difficult, and even dangerous, but it has to be done.

Without plumbing, our lives would be very different. We wouldn't be able to live or work in tall buildings. We couldn't take hot showers whenever we wanted. There would be more diseases. In many ways, plumbing makes modern life possible.

Getting to be a plumber isn't easy. It takes years of preparation. A student plumber, called an "apprentice," needs to be observant and careful. Having strong muscles also helps.

Today, we're going to learn about this important work from a person who has worked as a plumber for fifteen years. He will tell us stories about difficult problems that he's solved. Then, he'll answer our questions.

Now, let's welcome our guest speaker, Herbert the Plumber, who also happens to be my uncle.

JOB APPLICATIONS

Successful people often say that they began dreaming about their life's work as children. The following activity may start some of your students on the road toward great accomplishments.

DIRECTIONS:
1. Have the class brainstorm a list of jobs. These can be real or futuristic. (See suggestions in the margin.)
2. Ask students to choose a job they might like to pursue some day.
3. Have each student complete a copy of the job application form presented on the next page.
4. Students can share their forms in small groups.
5. Later, they might do a research report about the job.

EXTENSION:
Invite someone from an employment agency or from the school's personnel office to visit your class and talk about what he or she looks for when considering a job seeker.

Jobs
Accountant
Actor
Ad writer
Animal trainer
Artist
Banker
Business owner
Carpenter
Doctor
Electrician
Engineer
Farmer
Inventor
Lawyer
Letter carrier
Librarian
Mechanic
Musician
Photographer
Pilot
Planet tour guide
Plumber
Politician
Police officer
Programmer
Religious leader
Reporter
Sales person
Scientist
Soldier
Taxi driver
Teacher
Veterinarian
Writer

EMPLOYMENT ← OFFICE

Please Wait

Job Application Form

Application

1. Job: _____

2. Name: _____

3. Address: _____
   Number and Street
   _____
   City, State, ZIP code

4. Telephone number: _____

5. Give your reason or reasons for wanting this kind of job. If you need more space, use the back of this paper.

_____

_____

_____

_____

_____

_____

6. List any jobs, hobbies, skills, or other points that you feel are preparing you for this job.

_____

_____

7. If you have other comments, write them on the back.

MEMOIRS

The Greek goddess of memory (Mnemosyne) bore the nine Muses, who became patrons of literature, the arts, and sciences. Centuries later, many artists and scientists still teach that memory plays a vital role in creativity.

DIRECTIONS:
1. Read the memoir model on the next page. Explain that a memoir is a true story about a person, written from memory by a relative or a friend of the subject. Usually, the focus is an event, which can be ordinary (buying a car) or extraordinary (seeing a UFO).
2. Ask students to list friends or relatives who have had memorable experiences. These might relate to work, travels, hobbies, or other phases of life.
3. Each student should choose a subject and write a short memoir about a particular event in the subject's life.
4. Share the stories in small groups.

EXTENSION:
After students polish their memoirs, gather them into a class book.

Memoir Model

Uncle Abe's Snoring

My Uncle Abe used to come over to my house for dinner once a week. I always liked those nights because he was my favorite uncle. He was an electrician, so he could teach me all sorts of interesting things.

After dinner, though, he would usually fall asleep on the living room floor while he digested my mother's good cooking. As soon as his eyes closed, he would begin to snore. He was such a loud snorer, you could hear him all over the house. We told him many times about his snoring, but he always said he didn't do it, and that we were just making it up.

Then, for my tenth birthday, my parents gave me a tape recorder. I wasn't sure what I was going to do with it until, a few days later, Uncle Abe came over, ate, fell asleep, and started to snore.

I got the recorder, set the microphone right next to his mouth, and turned it on. My whole family came in to watch my uncle snore into the tape recorder.

When he woke up, I told him I had something for him to hear. I pushed the "play" button, and the sound of my uncle's loud snoring filled the room. His eyes widened as he recognized himself. I wasn't sure what he was going to do. Maybe he'd be angry with me. But then he started to laugh. It was a wonderful loud laugh. He couldn't stop even when I turned on the recorder. Later, when I played back his laughter, it made him laugh more than before.

PEN-PAL PEDAGOGY

Here's a letter-writing activity based on the ancient truth that "to teach is to learn twice." By teaching younger children, your students will deepen their own knowledge while taking pride in how much they have learned.

DIRECTIONS:
1. Ahead of time, find a teacher whose students can benefit from your students' advanced knowledge.
2. Have your students brainstorm their areas of expertise: academics, sports, hobbies, experiences, and general information.
3. Write a group letter to the other class offering to answer the younger students' questions. The letter might include a sheet or poster identifying your students' areas of expertise. (See the model on the next page.)
4. On another day, after questions arrive, have students, working alone or in small groups, prepare answers. These can be tested on the whole class before being "mailed." *Hint:* If both classes have computers, the letters can be sent via disk.

EXTENSION:
Collect the questions and answers into a class book, a copy of which can be donated to the library.

Information Sheet Model

If you have questions, we have answers!

The students in Room 226 want to share what they know with you. If you have questions about any of the following topics, please write us a letter. We'll answer you as soon as we can.

- Growing an indoor garden
- Drawing cartoon characters
- Writing haikus
- Juggling
- Making a simple telescope
- Tying knots
- Practicing the piano
- Having your appendix removed
- Performing magic tricks
- Housebreaking a dog
- Throwing and catching a football
- Speaking Spanish
- Putting on a puppet show
- Knitting a sweater
- Fixing a bicycle tire
- Doing a swan dive
- Reading a map
- Roller-blading
- Making an electromagnet
- Building model airplanes
- Visiting London, England
- Escaping from a burning house
- Taking photographs
- Baking an apple pie

We know even more than this list shows. Please send us any questions you have.

PHONE GREETINGS

In everyday life, the goal of an answering machine greeting is to entice callers to leave messages. But the same format can also be used to inspire imaginative writing, often with comical effect.

DIRECTIONS:
1. Have each student choose a favorite character from literature or history.
2. Ask students to write an answering machine message that might have been left by the character chosen. As with real answering machine messages, the greeting should:
   • Be about 30 words
   • Give a reason why the person isn't answering the phone
   • Invite callers to leave a message
3. Share the messages in small groups.

EXTENSION:
After editing their messages, students can "publish" them using the art frame on the next page. You might gather all the pages into a book of memorable phone greetings.

Hi, you've reached George Washington's phone. I'm at Valley Forge right now, but if you...

Phone Greeting

PRESS RELEASES

There's more news in the world than what's on CNN. Facinating occurrences happen close to home, but how will the world find out if no one says anything?

DIRECTIONS:

1. Hand out copies of the press release on the next page. Explain that many groups use this format to get publicity in newspapers and on TV. Go over the elements:
   - Date of the press release
   - Headline
   - Story with the five "w's": who, what, where, when, and why
   - Name of someone who can give more information
2. Brainstorm newsworthy events from the students' lives, or choose happenings from favorite fiction or nonfiction books.
3. Have each student, or pair of students, draft a short press release about an event.
4. Share the news in small groups.

EXTENSION:

Invite a reporter from a local newspaper to share press releases received by the paper, plus articles based on the releases. Or invite the publicity person from a local organization to teach a lesson on writing press releases.

Press Release Model

December 17

The Internet Comes to Boulevard School

In the last few days, students at the Boulevard School visited the White House, the Louvre Museum in Paris, Kennedy Spaceport, and a Hollywood movie studio.

You might think that the school discovered a gold mine. But all these visits cost nothing, thanks to the library's new computer, which is linked to the Internet. Students electronically traveled to home pages of these various places. There, they saw photographs and video, read announcements and fact sheets, and even got to post questions.

The computer was given to the school last month by the Parents and Teachers Association and by Computer Capers, a store located on Main Street. The phone company has donated a telephone line for the project.

You do not have to be a student to use the computer. Teachers are using it to prepare lessons, and Mrs. Irwin, the librarian, has invited interested parents to drop by to see what their children are learning with this amazing tool.

For more information, you can reach Mrs. Irwin at the school's main number: 555-7733.

QUERY LETTERS

Before building their first plane, the Wright brothers wrote to the Smithsonian Institution for information. Students can use the same research technique.

DIRECTIONS:

1. Explain that a query letter is a way of gathering information by writing to experts. Use the model on page 61 to illustrate the key elements:
   - Telling who the writer is
   - Stating the writer's question or questions
   - Thanking the expert
2. Choose a topic or have students choose topics for a query letter. Examples are:

topic	place to write
appendicitis	doctor
fire safety	fire department
lightning	weather bureau
presidential pets	White House

3. Have students draft short letters asking one or two questions relating to the topic.
4. Share the drafts in small groups.

EXTENSION:

Have students write query letters to collect information for reports. This could be the time to introduce the class to e-mail and to the Internet. See pages 92-95 for more information.

Query Letter Model

Post Office Box 457
Palo Alto, CA 94302
March 31, 1996

Murray Suid
1111 Greenwood Avenue
Palo Alto, CA 94301

Dear Mr. Suid:

I recently read your book <u>How to Be an Inventor</u>, which I enjoyed. I have many ideas for inventions, and your book may help me figure out how to actually make and sell them.

I'm writing to you about the story of the Slinky, which you told on page 45. The facts that you gave made me interested in learning more about that invention. Could you recommend a book or article that gives more information about that toy?

Also, do you have the address of the company that makes the Slinky? I have several questions which I would like to ask the company, for example, how the spring is made.

Thank you very much for your help.

Sincerely,

Irwin Hill

RECOMMENDATIONS

A letter of recommendation is a kind of advertisement for someone you know. Writing one for a friend can be a memorable gift.

DIRECTIONS:

1. Explain that to get into a college or to secure a job, a person may need letters of recommendation from friends, teachers, or others who know the applicant. This information might cover:
- Work habits
- Values
- Social skills
- Appearance and hygiene

2. Choose someone the students know about. It could be an historical figure or a fictional character.

3. Brainstorm a list of jobs that the person might be good at. For example, Jack, of beanstalk fame, might want a job as a telephone line person, or a trapeze artist.

4. Have the students draft letters explaining why the person would be just right for the job. For a model, see the next page.

EXTENSION:

Divide the class into pairs and have students write letters of recommendation for each other.

Recommendation Model

1 Safe Haven Way
Pigsburg
October 15

Owner
The Balloon Store
125 Main Street
Storyland

Dear Owner:

The Big Bad Wolf asked me to recommend him for a job blowing up balloons in your store.

I know Mr. Wolf quite well. If you need someone with a powerful breath, he is definitely the employee you are looking for. Not long ago, he huffed and puffed so strongly, he blew down two houses owned by my brothers.

I hope you will hire Mr. Wolf, because I think blowing up balloons would be a good use of his talent. I'd rather see him doing that job than blowing down houses.

However, if you have any pigs working for you, you should not hire him. Mr. Wolf has an appetite for pigs, wich could cause a problem among your workers. I do think Mr. Wolf gets along well with other wolves, and he probably would have no arguments with lions, tigers, crocodiles, sharks, or boa constrictors.

Please write me if you have any other questions about Mr. Wolf.

Sincerely,

The Third Little Pig

RESEARCH INTERVIEWS

Interviewing experts sharpens a variety of skills, such as asking questions, listening, and taking notes.

DIRECTIONS:
1. Have each student brainstorm a list of topics he or she has knowledge about. The list might cover skills, experiences, hobbies, and places visited.
2. Divide the class into pairs.
3. Have each student choose a topic from his or her partner's list and then write several questions about the topic.
4. Students should use their question lists to interview each other, taking notes as the information pours out (see the model on page 65).

EXTENSION:
Have students write articles based on their interviews and then publish the articles as a class-made encyclopedia.

Research Interview Model

Notes from an interview with Elro about pizza spinning

Q: Elro, how did you learn to toss a pizza?

A: My father taught me. He did it as a job in high school.

Q: What are the steps in tossing a pizza?

A: First, you make the dough. You put a package of yeast in a cup of warm water, mix in three cups of flour, knead the dough for five minutes, and let it rise for an hour in a warm place.

Q: Why in a warm place?

A: Yeast is a kind of plant. It needs heat to grow.

Q: I didn't know that. What do you do next?

A: Press the dough into a circle. You can do this with your hands or with a rolling pin. Then, make a fist with one hand and place the dough on top of the fist. Next, make a fist with the other hand and slip it under the dough. Gently move your fists in opposite directions and lower them quickly. This will spin the dough for a second before it drops onto the backs of your hands.

Q: Why not catch it with your fingers?

A: Fingers will poke holes in the dough. The trick is to keep spinning the dough until it spreads out. When it's big enough, you lower it onto a round baking pan, put on sauce, cheese, and other toppings, and bake it at 450 degrees Fahrenheit for about 12 minutes.

Q: It sounds easy.

A: Well, it takes practice. If you don't want to mess up a lot of dough, you can practice using a damp dish towel. If you can spin and catch the towel, then try to do it using dough.

RULES

Creating rules requires analytical thinking. It's an activity that can also raise awareness of the legal environment in which we live.

DIRECTIONS:

1. Brainstorm a list of rules and laws in the students' lives and discuss the reasons for having them:
   - To avoid conflict
   - To head off dangerous behavior
   - For efficiency

Note that a rule or law meant to solve one problem can cause other problems, as Prohibition did.

2. Give students a real or imaginary situation that requires rule-following. See the next page for topics.

3. Have students list as many rules as they can that might improve the situation.

4. Students can discuss their ideas in small groups.

EXTENSION:

Discuss the difference between a rule and a law (a law is enforced by a community). Have the class send ideas for laws to legislators at the local, state, or national level.

There ought to be a law...

There Ought to Be Rules for...

- Animals, if they could understand and follow rules, such as:
    - ants, mosquitoes, and other insects
    - cats, dogs, and other pets
    - cows, pigs, and other livestock
- Characters in famous stories such as:
    - The Cat in the Hat
    - "Cinderella"
    - "Goldilocks"
    - "Rumpelstiltskin"
    - "Snow White"
    - "The Three Little Pigs"
    - Where the Wild Things Are
    - The Wizard of Oz

- E-mail message senders
- Extraterrestrials visiting Earth
- Family members taking a long car trip together
- Guests at a birthday party
- Objects, if they could understand and follow rules, such as:
    - bar of soap
    - dishes
    - refrigerator
    - stove
    - television
- Parents meeting their child's teacher
- Passengers on spaceships going to other planets
- People who don't understand each other's language
- Plants, if they could understand and follow rules
- Time travelers:
    - from the present going to the past or future
    - from the past or future coming to the present
- Weather, if it could understand and follow rules, such as:
    - rain
    - snow
    - wind

SONG LYRICS

"Happy Birthday," "The Star-Spangled Banner," and many other songs were created by adding new words to old tunes. There's probably a hit inside of every student.

DIRECTIONS:

1. Give each student, or pair of students, a copy of the sheet music found on the next page.

2. Brainstorm themes for new songs using the old melody. Some possibilities are:

- Heroes
- Hobbies
- Homework
- Pets
- Sports

3. Have students write new lyrics that can be sung to the old tune. The old lyrics can serve as a guide to getting the rhythm right.

EXTENSION:

After students polish their lyrics, they can write them under the original words. You might make a book of "New Words to Old Tunes," or hold a "sing-in."

Sheet Music

STORY ENDERS

Some storytellers like to know how their stories will end before writing the beginnings. This strategy is an antidote to rambling, shaggy-dog tales.

DIRECTIONS:
1. Read aloud or write a story ender on the board (see page 71. Or hand out a sheet of picture story enders (pages 72 and 73) and choose one.
2. Explain that an "ender" is the final scene in a story that hasn't been written yet.
3. Have students think up a plot that leads to the given ending. They should describe the action in a few sentences or in a list of events leading to the final scene.
4. Ask students to share their plot summaries in small groups.
5. Later, students should use their summaries to draft short stories culminating in the action presented in the story ender.

EXTENSION:
Ask students to create their own text or picture story enders for use by their classmates. You might assemble a book of enders, which students can take home to try on their parents.

Sample Story Enders

The wolf came nearer and nearer. Its paws thumped noisily on the hard ground.

Now I could see the beast's huge teeth and even feel its warm breath. If I reached out, I could touch the beast's wet nose.

I stood perfectly still. Time seemed to stop. My breathing sounded like a roaring wind.

Finally, the hairy creature brushed against me, lifted its head, and gave my cheek a big, friendly lick. I laughed for joy. We were together once again, friends forever.

One more out and we'd be champs. Unfortunately, the other team's best batter was at the plate. Our pitcher nervously hurled the ball.

The batter took a giant swing. Crack! The ball rose in a high arc toward the fence. As I ran, I tried not to think of what happened last time, but the picture stayed in my head.

I looked up over my shoulder. The ball was coming. Suddenly, I remembered what Coach had said.

I smiled and stretched out my glove, and then felt the ball smack into the leather.

The clerk stuck out his hand, daring me to put something in it. I didn't smile. I didn't frown. I showed no emotion as I reached into my back pocket. A few coins jingled, but they meant nothing.

Finally, my fingers found the tattered piece of paper. I pulled it out and, without looking, slapped it into the clerk's palm. His eyes widened in disbelief.

"A thousand dollar bill," he whispered. He rubbed the paper.

"What did you expect," I said, "a hundred thousand pennies? Now give me the box, please."

I was amazed that so many people showed up. There were at least ten thousand in the crowd, maybe more. When they saw me, they chanted my name. Over and over they said it.

Finally, I lifted an arm and waved for them to be quiet. Eventually, they became silent. I adjusted the microphone, took a breath, and spoke.

"I don't deserve the credit," I said. "We owe our victory to the little ones."

I pointed to the fishbowl, in which the little ones were swimming.

"Give them your applause," I said. In response, there was a cheer so loud, it would have drowned out thunder.

THANK-YOU NOTES

Sending thoughtful thank-you notes is not only part of good manners, it also exercises creative thinking skills.

DIRECTIONS:
1. Teach the formula for the thank-you note:
   • Describe the gift
   • Tell how the gift will be used or why it is valued
   • Express thanks
2. Give students the Gift Cards sheet, page 75.
3. Have them pick out a gift they'd like to receive and then write a thank-you note.
4. Share the notes in small groups or post them on a bulletin board.
5. Use the cards for more practice. As a variation, ask students to choose a gift they would *not* like to get, and then write a thank-you note for it.

EXTENSION:
When someone does something nice for the classroom, have students write a group thank-you note. Or, have students look for special acts reported in the newspaper and then send a good Samaritan a thank-you note.

WALKING TOURS

Just as tour guides entertain visitors with informative speeches as they move around museums and other attractions, students can create tour presentations of places and objects in their lives.

DIRECTIONS:
1. Have students choose a familiar place that contains several interesting sights. For suggestions, see page 78.
2. Ask students to write a speech that could be used when taking people on a tour of the place. The description should name each sight and give a fact or two about it.
3. Students can share their tour speeches in small groups or, after revising them, post the tours on a bulletin board.

EXTENSION:
As an alternative to the traditional report, have students use the walking tour format. You'll find a model on page 77 and a list of suitable research topics on page 79.

My father likes to eat oatmeal. Also interesting is the wall clock, a gift from my uncle.

Walking Tour Model

Visit Your Amazing Teeth

How well do you know the 32 enameled tools called teeth? Do you understand what each is used for? If not, here's your chance to find out by exploring your mouth.

Those squarish, flat teeth at the front are called incisors. The word relates to "scissors" so you shouldn't be surprised that incisors are used for cutting. There are four upper incisors and four in the lower jaw.

On each side of the incisors is a single eye tooth, also called the canine tooth. The word "canine" means "dog."

On either side of the canines are two premolars, which have two raised bumps called cusps. If you move further into your mouth, you'll meet the next three teeth, which are molars. They look like premolars, but molars have four cusps. Premolars and molars are used for grinding and chewing.

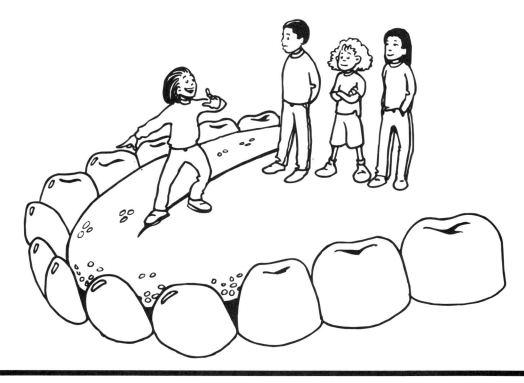

Familiar Places to Tour

Amusement park

Auditorium

Back yard

Bedroom

Book setting (e.g., island in Black Beauty)

Cafeteria

Church/synagogue

Classroom

Closet

Dentist's office

Doll house/model set-up

Face (own, classmate's)

Gymnasium

Junk drawer

Library

Movie theater

Musical instrument

Parent's workplace

Park/playground

Refrigerator

Relative's house (e.g., grandma's)

School bus

Shopping mall

Stadium

TV show setting

Zoo

Research Topics for Tours

Alimentary canal

Ancient cities, e.g., Julius Caesar's Rome

Battlegrounds, e.g., Gettysburg

Brain

Clock interior (old-fashioned escapement)

Computer

Contemporary cities

Dinosaur

Eiffel Tower

Factory

Fingerprints

Fruits (interior)

Gasoline engine (interior)

Lock (interior)

Moon

Ocean floor

Paper money (explain various symbols)

Pentagon

Pyramids (Egyptian, Mexican)

Rivers

Skeleton (human, animal)

Skyscraper (interior or exterior)

Space shuttle/space station

Spider web

Tree (interior or exterior)

Washington Monument

White House

WRITER'S GUIDE

Beginnings: The first sentence or first paragraph of a piece of writing is called the "lead" (pronounced "leed"). The lead should interest readers and give them a hint of what will follow. Most leads fit into one of the following types:

- Action leads show something happening, for example:
  The ball flew over my head. I turned to chase it.

- Character leads introduce one or more people,
  for example:
  Adelaide had the kind of smile that could make you sing.

- Quotation leads present someone talking, for example:
  "Where are you?" asked my sister. Her voice told me that something was wrong, but I couldn't tell what.

- One-word leads feature a single, powerful word, and then explain it in the next sentence, for example:
  Fear! That's what I felt as I heard the noise.

Conciseness: Writers should make every word count. Just as there should be no extra parts on a machine, there should be no extra words in a piece of writing. A first draft may contain unneeded words, but these can be trimmed during editing:

First Draft	Edited Draft
We did many fun things at the beach. We swam in the water, built castles out of sand, and got kites to fly in the wind.	At the beach we had fun swimming, building sand castles, and flying kites.

Descriptive writing: Descriptive writing should create a picture in the reader's mind. This doesn't mean that you have to use fancy words. Often a few simple details can create a mental picture.

Dialogue: The words spoken by characters can be the most interesting part of a story. Here are four dialogue examples:

- Use dialogue to move the action forward:
  "I'm going to look for gold," said Cyrus.

- Avoid ordinary expressions such as "Hi. How are you?" That works in real life, but it can bore readers. Instead, give your characters important words. For example:
  "Look out," she shouted. "It's an avalanche!"

- Have characters argue. Although arguments may be unpleasant in daily life, they add excitement to a story:
  "Turn left here," she said.
  "No. It's shorter the other way," he answered.
  She shook her head. "That leads to the swamp."

- For realism, have characters describe what they see:
  "Look over there, John."
  "What is it, Mary?"
  "Do you see that glowing light in the sky?"

Editing: Experienced writers improve their first drafts by editing (also called "revising" or "rewriting"). This involves moving words, adding details, correcting spelling mistakes, and making other changes. Here are two editing tricks:

- Read your work aloud to yourself. Make needed changes.

- Read your work aloud to someone else.

Endings: The following ideas can make endings memorable:

- Let the ending speak for itself. Instead of writing, "That's the end," try a dramatic image:
  My neighbors said nothing. They just looked at me and smiled. It was all the thanks I needed.

- Use an important or exciting idea in the last paragraph.
  Here's a final fact about the heart. During the average lifetime, this amazing pump will beat two billion times.

First draft: Some writers call the first draft a "rough draft." It's something like an artist's sketch. You don't have to get everything right the first time.

- If you're working on paper rather than a computer, skip every other line and leave wide margins. This way, you'll have room to make changes.

- Let your ideas flow. Don't be critical. An idea that seems weak may turn out to be useful after you think about it.

Ideas: Ideas are everywhere, but you need to use your eyes and ears to find them. Many writers keep an idea notebook or diary, in which they write down unusual observations that interest them. These observations later can be turned into stories, reports, or other kinds of writing.

- Keep track of your questions because they often serve as starting points for writing. Asking yourself "What if...?" can turn on your imagination.

- A strong emotional reaction to a subject can be a sign that you're thinking about something important.

Paragraphing: A paragraph is a section or part of a piece of writing. It usually consists of several sentences that deal with a single idea or action. Breaking a piece of writing into paragraphs helps readers follow the ideas or action.

- Indicate a paragraph by indenting the first line (moving it to the right).

- Watch paragraph length. Too many long paragraphs can slow or confuse readers. On the other hand, too many short sentences can make your writing seem choppy.

- In a story, start a new paragraph every time a character begins to speak.

Positive expressions: Sometimes, the best way to express an idea is with a negative phrase, for example: "I'm not afraid." In most cases, your writing will be clearer and more concise if you replace negative expressions with positive ones. For example:

Negative	Positive
not easy	difficult
not happy	sad
not real	fake

Pronouns: By replacing nouns, pronouns help writers avoid boring repetitions, such as "dog" in the following example:
> My dog is special. My dog can talk, but my dog's way of talking doesn't use words. My dog uses my dog's tail.

Here is the same thought expressed with pronouns:
> My dog is special. He can talk, but his way of talking doesn't use words. He uses his tail.

Make sure that each pronoun clearly refers to a noun. Otherwise, readers get confused and annoyed.

Sentences: Present your ideas in a series of clear sentences.

- Sentence length: Shorter sentences are usually easier to understand than longer sentences. If your goal is to be clear, your sentences should average about fifteen words. To maintain interest, mix short and long sentences.

- Sentence types: There are three kinds of sentences:
  Declarative sentences give information:
  > "Spiders have eight legs."

  Imperative sentences give commands:
  > "Be quiet."

  Interrogative sentences ask questions:
  > "Why blame me?"

Subject of the sentence: The subject of the sentence is like the main character in a movie. It's "who" or "what" the sentence is about. In most cases, your writing will be clearer if you put the subject at or near the start of the sentence.

Summary: When writing a summary, don't use the same words used earlier. Find a new way to express the ideas.

Title: A good title draws readers into your work.

- Make the title as specific as possible. "A Storm" is not as specific as "The Hurricane That Blew Off Our Roof."

- In most cases, make titles seven words or fewer.

- If you're writing about an event, try to include an action word in the title: "How I Painted Our Car...by Mistake!"

- If you're titling a story, consider including the main character in the title, for example: The Wizard of Oz.

Subject

Tools: Just as a carpenter or plumber needs tools to get a job done, a writer needs tools. These include:

- A dictionary: Use your dictionary to check on word meanings and spellings. Use it to find synonyms so you can avoid repetitious writing.

- Fact books: Use almanacs, encyclopedias, and other references to make your writing accurate. This is important even in fiction. For example, if you're setting a story in Miami, you don't want to tell readers that someone staying at a hotel there goes for a dip in the Pacific Ocean!

- A computer: Computers produce drafts that are usually easier to read than handwritten drafts. Also, because words written on a computer are easier to move around and change, editing becomes less of a chore.

Word choice: If you want your writing to be clear and interesting, you must carefully choose your words. Here are three hints about word choice:

- Never use a word you don't understand. If you're not sure, look it up in the dictionary or talk to someone about it.

- Use shorter words if you are trying to simplify your ideas:

longer word	shorter word
accomplish	do
lengthy	long
utilize	use
vehicle	car

This advice works only if the shorter word fits your meaning. If a longer word comes much closer to what you want to say, you should use the longer word.

- Choose specific words. Some words refer to many things. For example, the word "building" can refer to a store, a house, an apartment, a garage, a hospital, or a school. Usually, your writing will be stronger if you choose the word that comes closest to your meaning.

- Avoid accidental word repetitions. For example, if a first draft sentence reads, "I saw an electric saw in the hardware store," a careful writer might edit the sentence this way: "I noticed an electric saw in the hardware store."

- Make sure the words fit the assignment. For example, although you might use the the word "Hi " to start a letter to a friend, it would be better to use "Dear _____ " in a business letter.

HOW TO MAKE A BOOK

There are millions of books. But the most interesting book may be the one you publish yourself.

Step 1. Choose a subject. A book can be about anything in the world. This includes things in the world of imagination.

Step 2. Decide what kind of book you want to make. The two main types are fiction (books of make-believe stories) and nonfiction (books about real people, places, things, and happenings).

The Dog Who Went to College — Fiction

How to Do Circus Tricks — Nonfiction

Step 3. Know who your book is for. Do <u>you</u> want adults or little children to read your book? The audience you have in mind will affect all of your choices, including examples, illustrations, and wording.

Step 4. Do research. Sometimes you'll need to gather information about your subject. For example, if you're writing a story about a doctor, you may need to read about doctors or even talk to a doctor to make sure what you write is correct.

Is this the pet hospital? I'm writing a nonfiction book about dogs.

Step 5. Write the words. Some writers use paper and pencil. Others use a computer. Either way, after writing a first draft, most writers read their words and make changes so that the finished version will be clear and correct.

Step 6. Plan your pages. This is called "designing the book."

- **Lettering:** Decide how large to make the letters. If you use a computer, you can choose from different styles of type.

- **Page numbers:** Choose a place for the page number—top or bottom—at the corner or in the center of your page.

- **Title style:** If a page has a title, you need to decide how large the letters will be, and whether or not they will be boldface (dark and thick).

- **Margin width:** The margin is the white space on each side of the text. Usually, the margin will be an inch (2.54 centimeters) on each side.

- **Illustration:** Art can be photographs, drawings, even things taped or pasted on a page. When you design a page, decide how large the art should be and where it goes.

- **Spreads:** Some books present information in a two-page design called a "spread." If you plan to use spreads, then you'll need to print your pages on the back and the front.

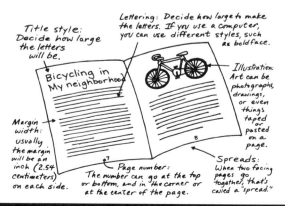

Title style: Decide how large the letters will be.

Lettering: Decide how large to make the letters. If you use a computer, you can use different styles, such as boldface.

Bicycling in My neighborhood

Illustration: Art can be photographs, drawings, or even things taped or pasted on a page.

Margin width: usually the margin will be an inch (2.54 centimeters) on each side.

Page number: The number can go at the top or bottom, and in the corner or at the center of the page.

Spreads: When two facing pages go together, that's called a "spread."

Step 7. Prepare the art. If you have a computer, you might be able to use a computerized drawing program to create the art.

Step 8. Carefully letter the pages. Don't forget to include the "front matter."

- The title page gives the book's title and the author's name.

- The copyright page tells when the book was written and names the company or group that is publishing the book.

- The contents page is found more often in nonfiction books than in fiction books.

Step 9. Design the cover. The cover not only protects the book but also invites people to read it. There are two covers—a front cover and a back cover. The front cover usually includes the title, the author's name, and a picture that gives a hint about the book's subject. Sometimes the front cover will also include a few words about what's inside.

The back cover is like an advertisement for the book. It usually contains a description of what's inside. If the book is nonfiction, the back cover may list some or all of the chapters or topics. The back cover may also give information about the author or authors.

Step 10. Combine the words and the art. Some computers allow you to combine words and art electronically. But if you don't have that kind of set up, you can do it with glue.

Step 11. Duplicate the pages and the cover. If you're going to make more than one copy of your book, you'll need to make copies of each page. Some copy machines make it easy to print on both sides of the paper. If you do this, be sure to use thick paper so that the words on one side can't be seen on the other side. The cover should be printed on thicker paper, sometimes called "cover stock."

Step 12. Bind the pages. There are many ways to bring the pages together to form a book. The easiest is to staple the pages and then cover the staples with binding tape (cloth tape) available in stationery stores. There are also machines that bind pages. You might find one in your school or at a photocopy store.

Step 13. Tell people about your book. A book comes alive only when people read it. One way to interest people in your book is to read part or all of it to them.

Step 14. Find a home for your book. You might give copies to the school and town libraries.

WRITING EVALUATION

A teacher's feedback can be a powerful force in sharpening writing skills. However, students must also learn to take responsibility for their own work.

Obviously, young writers aren't born knowing how to assess writing. One way to help them master this vital skill is to give them a checklist, such as the one on page 91. Students can use this form to take stock of their writing and their classmates' efforts as well.

The following notes on the checklist may prove helpful when you introduce it to the students.

Main idea: There's no one right way to express the main idea of any piece, be it "Hamlet" or a book report. Still, the evaluator should try to get the big picture before noting the details.

Title: The key is: Be specific. For example, "My Mom" is less interesting than "A Mom Who Flies."

Beginning: Point out that the beginning isn't just the "top" of the paper. A dramatic lead can win over readers. This is also true for the ending.

Sentences: Writing is usually smoother if sentences vary in terms of length, form, and function. (See the Writer's Guide, page 83.)

Wording: Two major pieces of advice are: Make every word count, and don't use words that you don't understand.

Paragraphing: Although there are some rules for paragraphing, deciding where to make breaks is partly a matter of taste.

Strengths and **Areas to improve:** These points help writers prepare for their next assignments. Stress the importance of making comments that are constructive rather than negative. This is obviously important when giving feedback to someone else, but it is equally important with self-evaluation. If students are too harsh on themselves, they can block their own progress.

Writing Evaluation Checklist

Title: _____ **Author:** _____

Type of writing: ( ) story ( ) report ( ) letter ( ) other: _____

Main idea: What is this piece of writing about? Use the back if needed:

_____

Title: Check each point that's true about the title:

( ) It's clear. ( ) It's specific. ( ) It's funny. ( ) Other: _____

Beginning: Check each point that's true about the beginning:

( ) It leads to the main idea. ( ) It's original. ( ) Other: _____

Ending: Check each point that's true about the ending:

( ) It supports the main idea. ( ) It's surprising. ( ) Other: _____

Sentences:

Have comma splices been corrected?	( ) yes	( ) none found
Have run-on sentences been removed?	( ) yes	( ) none found
Is there a mix of long and short sentences?	( ) yes	( ) no

Wording:

Have extra words been removed?	( ) yes	( ) none found
Have meaning errors been corrected?	( ) yes	( ) none found
Have repetitious words been deleted?	( ) yes	( ) none found

Paragraphs:

Were missing paragraph breaks added?	( ) yes	( ) none found
Were extra paragraphs removed?	( ) yes	( ) none found

Spelling and punctuation:

Have all misspellings been corrected?	( ) yes	( ) none found
Were wrong punctuation marks changed?	( ) yes	( ) none found
Were needed punctuation marks added?	( ) yes	( ) none needed

Strengths: Check each point that makes this piece of writing strong:

( ) Characters ( ) Facts ( ) Events ( ) Humor ( ) Other:_____

Areas to improve: What would have made this piece of writing better?

( ) More details ( ) More thrills ( ) More humor ( ) Other:_____

E-MAIL & THE WEB

Writing begins with observation, experience, and imagination. Fancy equipment isn't needed. Nevertheless, starting with the invention of papyrus, technology has aided language artists. Now we have e-mail and the World Wide Web. If you'd like to involve your students in these new tools, read on.

E-MAIL (ELECTRONIC MAIL)

BACKGROUND: E-mail is computer-to-computer pen-paling. The messages often travel over a computer network known as the Internet. Computers that send and receive e-mail are said to be "online." An online computer is equipped with a modem and communications software. The advantages of e-mail over traditional mail ("snail mail") are:

• E-mail can span the globe in minutes.

• You can receive e-mail seven days a week via any online computer. In effect, your mailbox travels with you.

• You can send an e-mail letter to many readers at once.

• E-mail costs about five cents a letter (even overseas), but you must subscribe to an online service for about $10 a month.

ACTIVITIES:

• Teach your students the grammar of e-mail. (See page 93.)

• If you have an online computer in school, encourage students to exchange e-mail with students around the country and abroad. This mail can involve school projects, for example, comparing weather or other local phenomena.

• If you have a computer that's not online, simulate e-mailing by exchanging electronic letters on disk with other classes.

THE WORLD WIDE WEB (WWW)

BACKGROUND: The WWW is an online electronic collection of text, pictures, movies, and sounds. No one owns it. All who want to share knowledge can do so provided they have an online computer and subscribe to a service that connects with the WWW.

ACTIVITIES:

• Give research assignments that require students to seek information on the Web. See page 94 for addresses.

• Create your own directory of worthwhile WWW sites. Share this information with parents, who can then explore the sites with their children at home.

Net Grammar

E-mail tends to be less formal and more playful than paper mail. It's also more interactive. To respond to your e-mail, you just click on an icon and type. The other person's address is automatically inserted. When you're done typing, one more click sends the letter on its way, arriving at its destination in minutes or seconds. People can exchange many e-mail letters each day.

To save time, but also to have fun, online pen pals often sprinkle their electronic messages with symbols and abbreviations. (Using all capital letters is the same as shouting.)

SYMBOLS
Symbols are made from punctuation marks and letters. For example, the smile is a colon : and a closing parenthesis).

:) = smile

:D = big grin

;) = wink

:X = my lips are sealed

:(= frown

:'(= crying

:-0 = yelling

ABBREVIATIONS

LOL = Laughing out loud

ROTFL = Rolling on the floor laughing

BRB = Be right back

BTW = By the way

Electronic Addresses

Every individual or group that sends or receives e-mail has an address. The U.S. President's e-mail address is: President@Whitehouse.gov

Those offering information on the World Wide Web have "home page" addresses. For example, the home page address of a group called "Childrens' Corner" is: http://www.citylimits.com/children

The home page is a table of contents listing articles, pictures, movies, games, and other resources. (See the "Children's Corner" home page on page 95.) Clicking words, bullets, or icons gives access to the material.

The Web contains thousands of home pages. A few examples are listed below. For more, look through a WWW directory at your public library. If you send us interesting e-mail or home page addresses, we'll post them for other teachers and parents. Our e-mail address is: mmbooks@aol.com

> Please Note: All the addresses start with: http://

Children's Literature Web Guide	www.ucalgary.ca/cal%>EdKbrown/
Children's Software Reviews	qv3pluto.leidenuniv.nl/steve/reviews/
DaVinci's Inventor Homepage (articles, contests, patent info, etc.)	leonardo-davinci.berkeley.edu/
NASA	www.hosc.mil/planet-earth/nasa.html
UFOs	ernie.bgsu.edu/~jzawodn/ufo/
Wacky Patent of the Month	colitz/com/site/wacky.htm
Weather Info Superhighway wxhwy.html	thunder.met.fseu.edu/%>Enws/

Note: We've tested each of the addresses above. However, electronic addresses typically become obsolete faster than traditional addresses.

Sample Home Page

Welcome to Children's Corner

Our Web site is family and child friendly. In the near future, we hope to bring you, the visitor, more stories, books, and articles that are relevant to the family today and in the future. We also intend to concentrate on bringing material that is fun and enjoyable to children and young people of our community.

Things to do on Our Corner

- Art & Drawings
- Books & Stories
- Fun & Stuff for Young People
    - Disney's Web Site
    - Interport's Kid Space
    - Carlos' Coloring Book
    - Family Explorer
    - Elementary Schools on the Net
    - Middle Schools on the Net
    - The Computer Museum!
    - Hypertext Webster's Dictionary Interface
    - Uncle Bob's Kids' Page
    - Kids' Web - A World Wide Web Digital Library for School Kids
    - Kids' Crossing
    - Kids on Campus, 1995
    - Learning Studio
    - The World Factbook 1994
    - Online Children's Stories
- Parenting Resources
- Student Activities
- Youth on Line

The Children's Corner is currently under construction. We hope to finish this portion of our neighborhood very soon. We also encourage parents and young people to send us comments or suggestions at Webmaster@citylimits.com

Thank you for stopping by.

BIBLIOGRAPHY

When books are used as models for teaching formats, the age level is not important. For example, Dr. Seuss's books have been used to illustrate story structure in college classes!

Anecdotes
And to Think That I Saw It on Mulberry Street by Dr. Seuss (fiction)
Casey at the Bat by Ernest Thayer (fiction)
The Day Jimmy's Boa Ate the Wash by Trinka Nobel (fiction)
Mr. and Mrs. Pig's Evening Out by Mary Rayner (fiction)

Autobiographies
Boy: Tales of Childhood by Roald Dahl
Homesick: My Own Story by Jean Fritz
I, Juan de Pereja by Elizabeth Borton de Trevino (fiction)
Tales of a Fourth Grade Nothing by Judy Blume (fiction)

Diaries
Anne Frank: The Diary of a Young Girl Hiding from the Nazis by Anne Frank
A Gathering of Days: A New England Girl's Journal by Joan Blos (fiction)

Dreams
Alice's Adventures in Wonderland by Lewis Carroll (fiction)
A Christmas Carol by Charles Dickens (fiction)
The Wonderful Wizard of Oz by Frank Baum (fiction)

Letters
Dear Mr. Henshaw by Beverly Cleary
Dear Peter Rabbit by Alma Flor Ada
The Jolly Postman by Janet and Allan Ahlberg

Memorable People (Biographical Stories)
Ben and Me by Robert Lawson (fiction)
The Bicycle Man by Alan Say
Sarah, Plain and Tall by Patricia MacLachlan (fiction)
Stevie by John Steptoe (fiction)